Yesterday's PAISLEY

by

Donald Malcolm

TO MY BELOVED WIFE, RITA
how she would have enjoyed this

WELLMEADOW STREET, PAISLEY

A view looking West, taken from the corner of Lady Lane (which is opposite the Coats Memorial Church). On our right is Waddell's photographic studio and two buildings up the street the shop's sign advertises ARTIFICIAL TEETH! In the far distance is the top of Well Street, with Charles Wilson, the butchers, under the awning on the right. The business changed hands about three years ago.

One of Paisley's landmarks for many years was the Four Square factory, where cigarettes and tobacco were manufactured and packaged with the distinctive four red squares. Dobie's business dated from 1809. Now dilapidated, their three-storey building of dado stucco designed by J. Steel Maitland of Paisley was once as dazzling white as swansdown.

INTRODUCTION

While it is unlikely, much as we might wish it, that there was an established Roman presence on the site that is now Paisley, it is possible that from time to time they passed this way. I like to think that they did.

In the 6th Century, Mirin, later canonised, set up a mission at the White Cart ford. And in 1163, the Abbey, one of the glories of Scotland, let alone Paisley, was founded. The Burgh Charter was granted in 1488.

The town has maintained a couthy independence and is famed for the Paisley pattern and the once-universal thread industry. (A mill set up in Petrograd before the Russian Revolution has just recently gone back into business.) There is a popular annual festival and many of the buildings have been cleaned up, although restoration of the integrity of County Square and made traffic-free, would be welcome — and a feather in some enterprising councillor's cap.

Paisley is a town of elegant skylines, everywhere you look. Our window on the world is through Glasgow Airport, ironically in Paisley. Our big city neighbours haven't managed to move the boundary ...

Poets, writers, artists, entertainers, actors, architects: Paisley has them all. Buddy or Ootlander*, we can be proud of our town.

In these pages we see some aspects of Paisley's history and activities that made the town worth keeping an eye on.

My thanks to Derek Malcolm; Ken Hinshalwood and Pauline McDougall (Renfrew District Libraries, Local History Department); Bob Grieves; Ellen Drummond and Eleanor Clark (J & P Coats — UK Ltd.) and David Rowand for assistance and information. Dr. Walker's book added another dimension to my text.

Donald Malcolm — June 1991

* Someone born between the Paisley boundary and Novosibirsk ..
or maybe even Petrograd ...

Robert Tannahill was born in Castle Street in 1774, but within a short time the family moved to this cottage in Queen Street. Robert worked as a weaver, but in his heart he was a poet, inspired by the local scenery. Tannahill was a great admirer of Burns, but did not always succeed in getting his own work published, a contributory factor to his suicide in 1810. This is a 1900s postcard view using an 1880s photograph, one of a number of such postcards of 'old' Paisley ... the marketing of nostalgia is not such a new idea.

THE CROSS, PAISLEY.

On its message side, this postcard bears the manuscript caption "Thomas Blakely was here 27th March 1912". Who was Thomas Blakely and what was he doing at the future site of the War Memorial? On the right is Gilmour Street and on the left is Moss Street. This stretch of Moss Street was recently gutted, re-built and had its facade cleaned and the work has certainly improved the appearance of the town centre.

4

2. Paisley War Memorial, Unveiled Sunday, 27th July, 1924

Above: This anonymously-published view which evidently shows the ceremony of laying the foundation stone of the War Memorial bears no caption. The publisher was not trying to be unhelpful towards posterity; he no doubt just assumed that the purchasers of his product would know all about the event being portrayed. Unfortunately, some years on, I have been unable to pin-point the date. Something is going on at Moss Street as a number of heads are turned in that direction. On the right, another photographer is at work. Big public events meant good business for them; after all, the more people in the photo the more potential sales from girlfriends, boyfriends, mothers.

Right: A War Memorial was first proposed in 1918, but a location was not chosen until 1923. The designer was Robert Lorimer and the dramatic bronze equestrian statue was the work of A. Meredith Williams.

How many photographs have we seen, with the spectators all too aware of the cameraman? Here, the young woman striding away is almost resolutely oblivious. The fine building with the balcony, on the corner of St. Mirren Brae and leading to Causeyside Street, still stands. The building on the right, once the home of Selway My Tailors and the Caledonian Railway Coy., is gone. The War Memorial stands on the site. The Paisley and District tram is advertising Cochran's, a famous Paisley store.

High Street. Paisley.

This is my favourite Paisley card — quite magnificent. Just look at the composition and the dozen-and-one interesting things to see. The white building (mid-left) is The Picture House. It degenerated into a bingo hall, but now the facade has been retained and a development of shops is being built behind it. This card re-inforces my contention that postcard photography has strong claims to being an art form. The unknown photographer showed much imagination and daring in recording a rainy day scene. I have several such cards. I like rainy days. Living in Paisley, that's just as well.

The Pen Corner. For long this was a famous landmark in Paisley High Street, on the corner of New Street. Opposite The Pen Corner is School Wynd with the Liberal Club at the bottom and the High Church at the top. The building at the right housed The Polytechnic, a large store. The top storey was removed in the 1980s.

8

High Street, Paisley.

Corsets, fish, photography and dentistry are just some of the services provided by the firms in this scene, looking East towards The Cross. The Liberal Club can be seen in all its glory; the tower is now truncated. The 1897 lamp standard is beautifully in evidence here. Just beyond the Liberal Club was the Globe Hotel. The hotel name can still be seen at the back of the building, to the right of School Wynd. Look at that motorcycle and sidecar tootling towards The Cross. A rendezvous with a lady, perhaps ...?

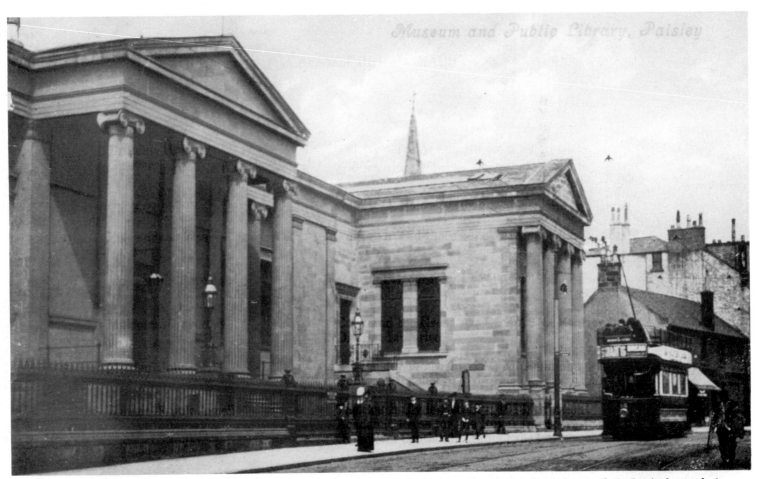

John Honeyman's magnificent buildings date from 1868 and 1881 and for those who don't know their Ionic from their Doric, the four columns of the portico are Ionic. Photographs of this group of buildings are invariably dull, without a cultural Buddy in sight — maybe they are all inside. This one shows a bit more imagination although there is some posing going on. The tram, advertising Gran's Bread, was serendipity at 13 miles an hour. Or did the photographer wait for it to come along? The High Church steeple can be seen, like the tip of a guided missile, above the Library. The ornate railings fell victim to the scrap iron drive in WW2.

West End Cross, Paisley

A scene that is much the same today as it was as seen here in 1906. The Coffin En', named for obvious reasons, has undergone various changes, but is still substantially unaltered and the clock tower is an enduring landmark. Paisley has many fine buildings, as can be seen in the tenement with the imaginative design of the facade. Generally, this area, which was run down for many years, has had a new lease of life.

Wellmeadow Street,   Paisley.

A marvellous card of a view substantially unaltered today. Dominating the skyline — Paisley is a town of fascinating skylines — is the dome of the John Neilson Institution (my first school) and the Thomas Coats Memorial Church. Yet another nostalgic touch in this West End scene: an early house in which I lived can be seen 'below' the globe of the lamp standard — Wellmeadow Post Office was downstairs.

12

WEST END CROSS, PAISLEY

The Royal Cafe was the current occupant of the lower portion of the Coffin 'En when this photograph was taken. The little edifice with the large lamp post was a public convenience — a favourite haunt of the inebriates from the nearby pubs. The main interest lies to the left; the then 'new' tenements can be seen behind the then soon to be demolished old buildings. The sign partially obscured by the lamp post reads The Vulcan Wine & Spirits Vaults.

Ferguslie Thread Works.

There is a Wellsian sweep and splendour to the buildings in this scene, with maybe a more sinister hint of Fritz Lang's *Metropolis*. Here was one of the highest concentrations of labour anywhere in Scotland and many people, mainly women, spent their working lives at Ferguslie. The Coats had been on the site since 1826 and during expansion in the 1880s Woodhouse and Morley of Bradford designed the Mills. Go there today and you'll find the area blanketed with houses. Only the ghosts remain.

14

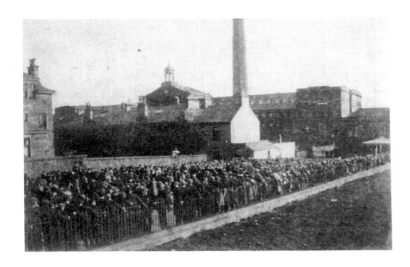

The Paisley Mill Girls Strike of September 1907 was sparked off by a strike in the spool-making department when the boys feared that the introduction of new machinery would lead to a reduction in wages. The girls at Anchor supported them, but the strike was sporadic and management retaliated by locking everyone out. At this point, Ferguslie Mills were unaffected and the Anchor girls determined to embroil the Ferguslie workers. These photos (from rather indistinct postcards) tell the story. Above left: The Anchor Mills workers arrive at Ferguslie. Above right: The Anchor Mills workers "persuading" Ferguslie Mills workers to join the strike (without success). Lower right: An attempt is made to rush the gates of Ferguslie Mills (some of the Ferguslie workers were injured).

The Ferguslie workforce was suspended on full pay until the strike was over.

DINNER HOUR
COATS MILLS, PAISLEY

See all those happy faces as the mill lassies — and some laddies — are shaken out like confetti into the sunshine and find some respite from routine. The Mills (Coats and Clarks) were once the town's biggest employers. The peak year was 1948, when 10,237 men and women were employed, 5,702 of them at Ferguslie. They all look as if they're in this scene, frozen in time. I once had the chance of a job with Coats. I was 16 and all I can recall was the glowing picture of my pension...

Both the Anchor and the Ferguslie Mills had fire services from the late 1870s and they supplemented the local fire brigade. Around 1880 the Mills had a 'steamer' — forerunner to the modern fire engines — and their equipment was superior to that of the Council. The Mills also had sprinkler systems. Initially the Mills brigades had a Fire Captain and two Lieutenants. The title of Fire Master came in later. Industrial fire fighting was a reserved occupation, which accounts for the fact that only five of the men in this photograph are wearing war medals, pointed out to me by Richard Mathieson. The equipment seen here was manufactured in Milan and it would be good to think that it has been preserved somewhere.

County Square   PAISLEY

This majestic building was on the opposite side of the square to the Post Office with the entrance to the old prison at the right of the picture. This castellated symphony in stone existed from 1818 until 1968, when it and the prison were demolished by the Town Council in their role of official vandals. The replacement was the quaintly-named Piazza — in Walker's words 'a vastly vulgar development of shops and offices' ... an 'open sore'. I've seen more attractive building sites. As I recently suggested, the integrity of the square should be restored. It could be done if someone had the will and the imagination, but that is patently lacking.

38   PAISLEY MUNICIPAL BUILDING

Here are the municipal buildings again, this time in festive mood for the Coronation of King George VI and Queen Elizabeth on 12th May 1937. It is sad that such Baronial splendour was lost. A short-sighted Council didn't appreciate what a treasure it had so casually caused to be demolished. The next time that you are in County Square, see the building in your imagination.

PAISLEY POST OFFICE

The Post Office, a fine sandstone structure in County Square, is the work of W.W. Robertson, 1892-93. It was official-ly opened on St. Valentine's Day 1893. It is seen here circa 1907, prior to the addition of Oldgrieve's 1912 wing (described by Walker as Glasgow Style Baronial). It looks so peaceful. Today, County Square is a mad-house, in-variably snarled with traffic and hectoring taxis and it is no pleasure to walk here. Perhaps some bright councillor might get something done about it someday.

Gilmour Street Station (1887) forms one side of County Square. The foundation stone of the ashlar viaduct was laid in September 1838 and the line was opened in July 1840. On the back of this postcard is the printed legend: Co-operative Congress, 1905 "KEEP YOUR EYE ON PAISLEY". The quotation is from a Disraeli novel *(Sybil?).* The Co-op, as it was universally known, was for many years a powerful force in Paisley.

At the left of the scene is the Sheriff Court: 'A symmetrical two-storey palazzo with real presence, projecting end bays are joined by a balconied Roman Doric loggia.' — Walker, again. The architects were Clarke and Bell and it dates from 1885. The adjacent County Buildings (1890), now the Procurator Fiscal's Office, is by them also. This one has an 'off-centre Ionic temple' and very imposing the buildings are. When this photograph was taken, there was still a public convenience at the end of St. James Street — maybe the authorities realised that the experience of attending the Sheriff Court might be too much for some of the local villains? Beyond it is the Holy Trinity Church, now, due to road changes, sitting in heavenly isolation.

This busy scene is taken from the South, looking towards Paisley Cross in the 1930s. The buildings on the right are still there. The large building on the left, the Russell Institute, was undergoing repairs at the time of the photograph. The splendid design by Paisley architect J. Steel Maitland was a fitting memorial gifted to the town by Miss Agnes Russell to mark the contribution to the development of Paisley by her late brothers, both solicitors. The clinic, which initially catered for mothers and their young children, was officially opened by H.R.H. Princess Mary on 19th March 1927.

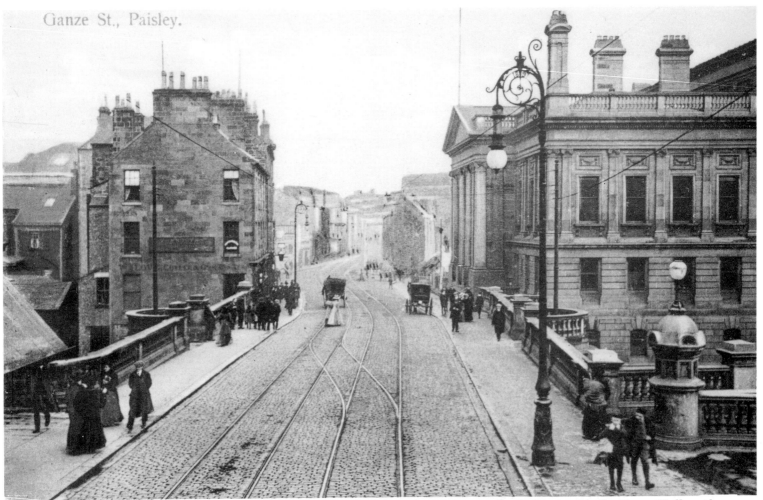

Ganze St., Paisley.

A printer's error renders Gauze Street as 'Ganze Street'. This early 1900s view looks East with the Town Hall on the right; much beyond it has been demolished. The name on the building on the left seems to be Wm. Love and the card was published by William Love, Wholesale Stationer of Glasgow — coincidence or a relation? This side of the river is now lost, like the Styx, under another Council-inspired disaster — the Piazza. Give Paisley back its river!

East Toll, Paisley.

The distinctive Old Toll House (James Donald, 1895-96), here seen circa 1906, once stood on the corners of Incle and Gauze Streets. Sadly, the official vandals had their way and it was demolished to make way for a road. The buildings on the left are also long gone and the area has been blighted by county and regional offices. Note the ornate lamp standard celebrating Queen Victoria's Diamond Jubilee in 1897.

Crossflat Terrace and McKerrell Street, Paisley

A busy scene towards the East end of the town! The main road runs across the middle distance; to the right leads to the Cross and to the left — foreign parts, such as Glasgow. The shop on the corner of the tenement was the Co-op and the Grammar School is on the opposite side of McKerrell Street.

Sherwood Church, Paisley.

James Donald, a Paisley architect, designed this Free Church which celebrates its centenary in 1991 — or rather, most of it does. The 120 ft. tower was demolished in 1987, thus removing a landmark from the town's East End. This postcard, used in 1910, shows the fine open setting of the church. The tenement remains. To the left, beyond the railings (now gone), is the Grammar School. In May this year an exhibition of flowers and photographs, 'The Ten Decades of Sherwood', was held in the church.

Maxwellton Park, Paisley.

An idyllic scene from yesteryear, South-West of the town and just off the main road to Elderslie and Johnstone. The white building (shelter and toilets) is gone, as is the factory seen in the background. The park now has tennis courts and a bowling green. The factory (Glenfield Works) was the premises of Wm. Wotherspoon, a subsidiary of Brown & Polson, and produced Glenfield flour and starch.

Tennis Courts, Barshaw Park, Paisley.

Barshaw Park was opened to the public in 1912 and lies North of the main road to Glasgow at the East End of Paisley. It includes a nursery, gardens, tennis courts and a boating pond from which an uncle of mine once rescued a young boy. The nearer part of the wooden buildings at the left contained the booking office and led to the tea rooms. Camphill (and maybe other schools) used to hold its tennis competitions here and on one occasion, I reached the nadir of my tennis career, conceding three straight aces in one game.

This view looks south from Love Street towards Caledonia Street, with the chimneys of factories such as McKean's Starch Works and engineers A.F. Craig (now both long gone) on the skyline. The original area, known as Hope Temple Gardens, was purchased by Thomas Coats in 1866. Two years later, on the anniversary of Queen Victoria's birthday (May 26th), the Fountain Gardens were handed over to the Town Council. A fountain with a sense of humour (it has four walruses!) sits at the centre and is the work of Ironfounders G. Smith and Company. Gazing down on the walruses is S.W. Pomeroy's statue of Robert Burns, who no doubt is thinking up some pithy rhyme.

30

This is a new P.C. just The "Glen" Concert Gleniffer Braes, Paisley.
out to day. *shows Thousands of People, taken last concert day.*

Talk about the hills being alive with the sound of music! The concerts were held on the Gleniffer Braes and fall into three periods: 1879-1889, 1893-1916 and 1924-1935. Disease might have caused the first break — McCarthy cites the 1880s as the peak period for both typhus and enteric fever, while the Great War and its aftermath probably account for the second. You can see the message on the front of this 1906 McDougal Brothers postcard: 'This is a new P.C. just out to-day. Shows Thousands of People, taken last concert day.' Actually, the photo most probably dates from 1901.

Technical School, Paisley.

Yet another Paisley benefactor was Peter Brough, a Perth businessman who, at his death in 1883, left about £155,000 to various bodies and causes in Paisley. As a result of one of these bequests, the Technical School was established. The building, at 42 George Street, was by Abercrombie. The site was provided by Coats, whose School of Design was incorporated in the Technical School. Since its inception, my alma mater has expanded considerably and has a worldwide reputation. Current Government thinking on higher education might mean the conferring of university status.

This was one of Paisley's three famous schools, built on an imposing site. It was designed by Paisley architect Charles Davidson and when it was opened in 1888, the original name was to be Victoria School because the Queen had visited the town in that year. However, Camphill, after the area, prevailed. Well I remember my first day, toiling up to the school. My father (who died at 93) was one of the first pupils and he recited this piece of doggerel:

Oor wee school
Is a great wee school
It's built o' bricks and plaister
The only thing that's wrang wi' it
Is the baldy-heided maister.

Sadly, the school, which had a magnificent literary mural in the main hall, was demolished in 1969 and replaced with a drab and functional school called Castlehead. The Camphill name was transferred to another equally uninspired concrete pile.

If you leaned on the railings at the front of Camphill, there, across the town, like a challenge standing atop Oakshaw, was the Neilson — the JNI — looking almost ecclesiastical with its great dome (hence its local name — the Porridge Bowl). It was opened in 1851 as the result of a bequest from John Neilson, a Paisley grocer. The aim of the school was to provide education for what are euphemistically termed today underprivileged children. The John Neilson was closed in 1978 and yet another ugly concrete heap was given the proud name. The JNI is a listed building — so couldn't be knocked down — and a £1.6m luxury development is now proposed.

37755 JV. GRAMMAR SCHOOL, PAISLEY.

The Charter of the school was granted in 1576 during Morton's regency for the 10-year old James VI and some of the revenues of St. Mirin's shrine were used to establish it. The curriculum was classical and the school's purpose was to provide scholars to the universities. It has been on four different sites. The present school, which now has an extension, is seen here and dates from 1891. Its proper title is The Paisley Grammar School and William B. Barbour Academy, Mr. Barbour having generously provided the money for its design and construction.

Clark's was the other very well-known thread firm in Paisley. The pavilion, once the home of the Anchor Recreation Club serving the members of the Anchor Mills, was designed by T.G. Abercrombie and it was officially opened in 1923. My personal memory of the ground is of winning the 220 yards for Sanda House in the Camphill School sports of 1949. Truth to tell, two faster runners shot off the final bend while I managed to hug it and break the tape. I have the photograph to prove it too!

This photo was taken on the occasion of the Annual Bowling Match, at Anchor Grounds, on Tuesday 10th May 1938, between J. & P. Coats Ltd. Finishing Divisions 2/5 and UTM (United Thread Mills) Ltd. Finance Department. On the back of the photo, all the names are listed with 'deceased' written in pencil against seven names. If any of them are still alive, they must be a great age.

SCOTTISH CROSS COUNTRY TEAM 1921.

The athlete with the no.27 shirt was a famous Paisley man, David Cummings, who competed for Britain in the 3,000 metres steeple-chase in the 1924 Paris Olympics. Eric Liddell was in the team and himself won lasting fame in the 400 metres (as featured in the film *Chariots of Fire*). Liddell visited David at his home in Neilston Road, Paisley and it was somehow strange to be in that same room holding the large medallion that David received, with as it were, Liddell's ghost present. I was coached by David as a member of Paisley Harriers.

Anchor Mills V.A.D. Red Cross Fête, held in the grounds of Anchor Bowling Club, 11/9/15.

The scene of the fete was the Anchor Bowling Club grounds and it was well-patronised on what looks like an Indian summer's day. The Voluntary Aid Detachment would be composed of the ladies of the town, engaged in raising funds to send comfort to the troops. Ten days after this photograph was taken, the Battle of Loos began with the customary artillery bombardment. Perhaps some of the intended recipients of the parcels didn't live to get them.

Having a "High Old Time" at Paisley

Comic and cartoon cards (this and opposite page). The Brodie Park card and fresh 'air from Paisley are simply standard cards with the Paisley reference overprinted. Similar cards exist for other places. The same applies to the mock aeroplane over The Cross, with the Coats looking askance. The publishers were cashing in on the immense popularity of aviation during the pioneer years of 1903-14. The Alexandra Infirmary card was used on 17th May 1919, but was possibly produced during the Great War as a convalescence card for those soldiers not too seriously wounded.

IT IS NO CRIME TO KISS, IN

BRODIE PARK PAISLEY

"To Err is human, to kiss, divine"

A little fresh 'air from PAISLEY.

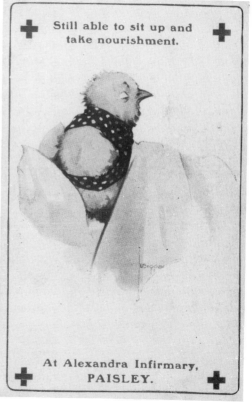

Still able to sit up and take nourishment.

At Alexandra Infirmary, PAISLEY.

ROYAL ALEXANDRA INFIRMARY
PAISLEY

Affectionately known as the RAI, this magnificent building (in E-plan) was the work of T.G. Abercrombie, from 1896 to 1900. Walker can't decide on the exact style of Abercrombie's 'inventive exuberance', so I shan't attempt a description. The RAI won't see its centenary as a hospital as it was recently closed and is now effectively screened from Neilston Road by a reasonably tasteful housing development. At the time of writing (May 1991), the exterior is festooned with scaffolding. It's to be hoped that the building doesn't become yet another bureaucratic hideout.

DRILL HALL, PAISLEY.

Abercrombie's polychrome sandstone Scots Renaissance building with an Art Nouveau bellcote (1896) replaced the original hall of 1865 and was for long associated with the Argyll and Sutherland Highlanders. It sits to the right of the museum complex and opposite the Paisley College of Technology. Note the posters, one of which states Recruits Wanted. The two cannons in the scene were presented to the town as the result of a letter from Lord Panmure at the War Office dated 28th April 1857. I seem to recall that Lord Cardigan was actually responsible for the gesture. Incredibly, these Russian guns apparently 'disappeared' during the WWII scrap iron drive.

43

OBSERVATORY, PAISLEY.

453.

Paisley benefitted from the largesse of a number of rich and influential men. The Coats family gave the town its fine observatory. I can do no better than quote Walker's description: 'Honeyman's Coats Observatory (1883) beautifully executed channelled and polished ashlar with a great Doric frieze and cornice supporting a balustrade around the observation drum'. He almost makes the stones speak. Among the excellent instruments is a Grubb 10″ refracting telescope. The orrery shows the motions of only eight major planets as Pluto (not discovered until 1930) was unknown when it was constructed. Note the wireless mast.

44

Ferguslie Half Time School, Paisley.

This was usually known simply as the Half Timers' School and it was one of the many paternalistic gestures by the Coats firm, in this instance to provide education to children of the mill workers. Bradford architects Woodhouse and Morley, who designed the majestic mills, were also responsible for the school (1887) and they didn't half let themselves go! Walker describes it as the architects' 'most ornate brick and ashlar Renaissance, absurdly flamboyant...'

Left: Of most interest here is the building seen partially at the left — the Glen Cinema. It was there, on Hogmanay 1929, that the dreaded cry of *"Fire!"* led to panic. Seventy children perished and ironically there had been no fire. A piece of film had caught alight, but the operator put it out. He then placed the reel outside the projection room. The smoke seeped into the auditorium, with tragic results. In another touch of cruel irony, this card was posted just three days before the tragedy wishing its recipient 'a happy New Year'.

Right: The dedication ceremony of Sunday 27th July 1924. The photographer of this scene took his shot from an upstairs window in Moss Street and included the sign of the Royal Animated Pictures, above the entrance to the Good Templar Halls, in Gilmour Street. The Glen Cinema is just out of the scene, to the right.

The Cenotaph, Paisley.

Left: Scotland's Bard had a strong association with Paisley through his marriage to Jean Armour and the Paisley Burns Club, founded by Tannahill and a group of weaver poets, was one of the first to be formed. Pomeroy's statue stands in the Fountain Gardens and was unveiled by Lord Roseberry in 1896. At the time, various other sites had been proposed and rejected. A few years ago, there was talk of moving Rabbie to another site, but nothing came of it and I think that he is happy where he is with his memories of Paisley, especially of the years of WWII, when the Gardens were a favourite haunt of American servicemen and their local girl-friends.

Right: Hugh MacDonald (1817-1860) was one of Paisley's better-known poets and yet I consulted several books on Paisley, including the one published for the 500th anniversary of the Charter, and found no mention of him. There also seems to be confusion on whether it is 'Mc' or 'Mac'. *The Bonnie wee well on the breist o' the brae* is engraved on the present memorial, which dates from 1883. The first one, provided by the Glasgow Ramblers Club (he'd written a book, *Rambles Around Glasgow)* was vandalised; the members promptly took it back and re-sited it on Glasgow Green. I wonder how it has been doing there? Paisley councillors are seldom absent from the pages of the local press, often targets of complaint and on the centenary of the unveiling 'A. Buddie' was giving them the edge of the tongue about the dilapidated state of the well.

Burns Statue, Paisley.   RELIABLE [WR &S] SERIES.

MacDonald's Well, Gleniffer Braes, Paisley.   RELIABLE [WR &S] SERIES.

Most postcards give the area its correct name, Dunn Square, after William Dunn who bequeathed the money. The Square was laid out by Paisley architect James Donald and formally opened in 1894. The Queen's statue was erected in 1901. The buildings in the background have long since been demolished, the site re-developed and the War Memorial now stands in the area 'between' the statue and the turreted building. The statues on either side of the steps are of Thomas and Peter Coats and are by Birnie Rhind (1889). Erected in 1910 at the foot of the steps was the Dunn Fountain which Walker describes as 'a bronze mother and child group faintly charged with Art Nouveau eroticism'. In *Paisley!*

48

Dunn Square and Causeyside Street, Paisley

... and here *is* that naughty statue, surrounded by the innocence of youth. The facade of the Co-operative Buildings on the right has been retained and in behind will be a new shopping centre, due to open in Spring 1992. The topping-out ceremony took place in June 1991. The buildings beyond the statue, at the bottom of Dunn Square, have been suitably renovated and are presently occupied by a bank, a solicitor and a hi-fi firm.

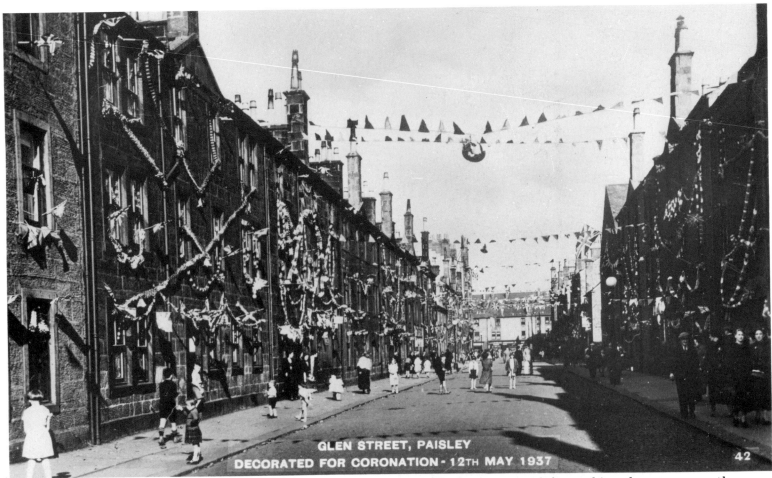

GLEN STREET, PAISLEY
DECORATED FOR CORONATION - 12TH MAY 1937

42

Paisley had a great tradition of street decorations, which was really the preserve of the working classes as were the back-door concerts which I can remember from when I lived in Caledonia Street (which runs at right angles to the south end of Glen Street). The message on the back of this lovely scene comments: 'It puts some of the artistocratic quarters in the shade'. The buildings seen here were demolished and the site re-developed for modern housing. Incidentally, there used to be a grandly-named Glen Street Gang, whose members were not actually all that tough. They probably saw too many Cagney films.

HIGH STREET, PAISLEY

1953 and Paisley is draped in bunting again in this view looking towards The Cross. The High Street has many fine buildings, but I wonder how many people pause to look up? Above 'Paisley' can be seen a building swathed in a large banner — The Picture House. Gary Cooper's name is on the canopy and the film showing was *High Noon*.

The earliest reference to a fire service is of two fire engines in the Council's possession in the 1760s, but they were not considered efficient enough and several 'of the principal inhabitants of the town' put up the money for a larger one to preserve the 'town from the danger and hazard of fire'. The new engine, complete with a leather pipe, was to be sent from London by sea. By 1800, there were two fire engines, one steam and one manual, kept at the Meat Market, in Weigh-house Close, High Street. This elegant Model T Ford engine dates, I think, from the early 1920s.

THE ENTRANCE INFECTIOUS DISEASE HOSPITAL, HAWKHEAD, PAISLEY. A.6414.

Now partially closed, the hospital was designed by Thomas Tait, a Paisley architect who also designed most of the 1938 Empire Exhibition pavilions at Bellahouston. The Tower of Empire usually sticks in most folk's minds as Tait's Tower. There is current discussion in Glasgow about something that would be identified with the city. The answer is obvious: re-build Tait's Tower! In Sydney, the decorative abutements of the mighty Harbour Bridge (the world's second-largest steel arch bridge) were designed by Tait.

53

163.

This is a card from a set or series of broodingly atmospheric, almost Gothic scenes, not far from the present Glasgow Airport, on the back road to Inchinnan (home of the R34). Barnsford Bridge, which actually crosses the Gryffe, was built in 1793. The Town Council contributed £100 towards its construction and they were 'assignees on this road, along with the other trustees, for making and repairing the same' (Council Records, 21st January 1793). A modern bridge now replaces the old bridge. The distinctive building was the Walkinshaw Brick Works, long since out of use.

54

No.541, a Black Stanier Five, 4-6-4T, of the Glasgow & South Western Railway, thunders out of Gilmour Street Station in June 1922. She was the 12.30 St. Enoch to Stranraer. This photocard catches the thrill and the excitement, but not the smoke and the grime, of the age of steam!

A SELECT BIBLIOGRAPHY

Brotchie A.W. and
Grieves R.L.

Paisley's Trams and Buses: 2 volumes:
Eighties to Twenties, 1986
Twenties to Eighties, 1988; N.B. Traction, Dundee

Clark, Sylvia

Paisley: a History; 1988; Mainstream Publishing

England, Valerie

Paisley in Old Picture Postcards; 1983; European
Library

McCarthy, Mary

A Social Geography of Paisley; 1969; Paisley
Public Library

Malcolm, Donald

Cody and the Great Air Race; 1978; Renfrew
District Libraries

Malden, John

Let Paisley Flourish; 1991; Museum and Art
Galleries, Paisley

Walker, Frank Arneil

The South Clyde Estuary; 1986; Scottish
Academic Press for the Royal Incorporation of Architects in Scotland, Edinburgh.